"Who am I to Write a Book?"

You CAN write a book to build your business

by Lynne Klippel

Copyright ©2007 Lynne Klippel

All rights reserved. Excerpt is permitted under the United States Copyright Act of 1976; no part of this publication may be reproduced or distributed in any form or by any means, or stored in a data base or retrieval system, without the prior written permission of the publisher.

Published by
MP Press
A Division of Femme Osage Publishing
St. Peters, MO 63376
636-922-2634
www.FemmeOsagePublishing.com

ISBN: 978-0-9728940-9-8

Library of Congress Control Number: 2007900409

First printing: 2007

Printed in the United States of America

Cover Design by
Cyanotype.ca

Proofreading by
Shirley Buschena

Dedication

To Robbie, Tommy, and Jake, who never let fear stop them from anything.

Thanks for teaching me bravery.

Acknowledgements

Thanks go out to all the business people I've met over the last few years who've shared their dreams and fears about writing a book. You inspired me to write this one.

To all the students of Book School and individuals whom I've had the priviledge of coaching and publishing, thank you for trusting me with your books and giving me the chance to read it first! Your questions and enthusiasm spark my creativity on a daily basis.

Lastly, but most importantly, my deepest thanks to my partner in life and business, Larry Klippel. Your technical expertise, love, and constant support make it possible for me to soar. Thanks, Sweetie!

Table of Contents

Dedication	i
Acknowledgements	ii
Introduction	1
Do you want to write a book?	3
Why Write a Book?	7
Why write a book in the first place?	9
Section 1	15
What are Strategy Barriers?	17
I can't write well enough to be an author	19
It will take me too long and cost too much money to write my book	21
The mechanics of writing are beyond me	25
My book has to be perfect or it is a failure	27
There are too many books about my topic on the market already	29
To write a book, I have to know what I stand for and I'm not sure I really know what I stand for	33
I don't know where to start	35
Section 2	37
What Are My Belief Barriers?	39
I'm not smart or degreed enough	41

Who am I to tell other people what to do?	47
Writing is hard and lonely	51
No one but my mother will read my book	55
I'll be ridiculed and humiliated if I write this book	57
I'll become famous and be overwhelmed by reporters and paparazzi who will stalk my every move for the morning papers	59

Solutions and Strategies — 63

Strategies You Can Use — 65

Get support	67
Set a date publicly, Be bold	71
Write daily	73
Read great books	75
Understand the publishing process	77
Select your topic wisely	79

The Next Steps — 87

So, are you convinced? — 89

Bibliography — 91

Resources — 92

About the Author — 93

Introduction

Who am I to Write a Book

Do you want to write a book?

You are not alone. In fact, a recent study found that 80% of us want to write a book to share our wisdom, leave a legacy, or grow our business.

Have you started your book yet?

Have you finished it?

If you haven't, you are not alone there either. The goal of writing a book seems so big, so impossible, that few of us actually find the time and courage to begin, let alone complete, the book of our dreams.

In fact, in my research and experience teaching writing over the past few years, I've found that there are common reasons why we don't write books. There are thirteen of them.

I call these thirteen reasons "The 13 Book Barriers". They are the excuses our minds use to stop us from writing the books of our dreams. Like a cloud of angry mosquitoes, they buzz around our heads and keep us stuck in wishing, not in writing.

These barriers fall into two categories: strategies and beliefs.

Here's some great news:

Once you identify these thirteen barriers and realize that they are not true, you can write your book! I've observed hundreds of authors overcome these barriers, and wrestled with them myself.

In this book, I'm going to dissect the thirteen book barriers, show you why they are not true, and give you the confidence you need to get busy on your book.

Then, I'm going to provide you with some solutions that will help you overcome them easily.

You'll notice that none of these barriers sound unfamiliar. You've heard them in the back of your mind for a long time. After you've finished this book, you'll have some new information to quell your internal doubter.

To get the greatest benefit from this book, answer the questions in each section. Each question is specifically designed to help you clarify your thinking and reduce your concern about writing.

While you use this book, you will be serving as your own writing coach. You may be surprised at the discoveries you make!

Enjoy the process,

Lynne Klippel

Why Write a Book?

Why write a book in the first place?

◇◇

There are many kinds of books and many reasons to write them.

However, in this work, we will talk about a very specific type of book, a Business Building Book.

In 2001, I met a very professional fellow at a seminar. He was a consultant to accounting firms who wanted to get more clients. As we concluded our chat, I asked him for his business card.

His next statement was unforgettably impressive.

He said, "Oh, Lynne, I don't carry business cards any longer. Let me give you a copy of my latest book instead."

Imagine my shock when he pulled a book out of his briefcase, autographed it with a flourish, and handed it to me.

Wow.

He told me later that he gave his book away everywhere he went, on airplanes, at meetings, even at his doctor's office. His book provided basic sales information useful to any small business owner.

When I asked him why he gave his book away to people who were not accountants, he laughed. He reminded me that every business person had an accountant or knew one.

This book, <u>The I Hate Selling Book</u> by Allan Boress, lead to many referrals and consulting gigs for my new acquaintance. In fact, he now teaches selling techniques to service providers all around the globe.

What if the owner of your favorite restaurant handed you a book of recipes?

What if an attorney gave you a book of tips to help you select the right attorney for your needs?

What if your home insurance salesman gave you a book with ways to protect your home from fire damage?

What if a life coach gave you a book of stress reduction strategies?

Business Building Books create customer loyalty, introduce people to your information before you ask them to purchase anything, and showcase your expertise. They also generate word-of-mouth advertising and referrals.

When you open a small business, it can be difficult to get attention from the media. Your press release about your grand opening or special sale may not make the news.

However, when you are an author, you can create a press release that shares specific, useful information. Now you are no longer talking about your business, you are providing content.

If you were a reporter, which headline would interest your listeners more?

Sale at Jones' Dry Cleaning today

Or

Author reveals 5 ways to make your expensive suits last longer

Can you write a Business Building Book?

Yes, you can if you know how to present your knowledge in a useful and entertaining fashion, and you are willing to invest a bit of time and effort in the process.

Before we address some of the barriers you may be hearing in your head right now, dream a little bit.

What could a book do for your business?

Do any of your competitors have a book?

What would your prospects or ideal customers like to learn from you?

What creative ideas does this topic spark in you right now?

Creating a Business Building Book can be a profitable way of growing your business. When you have a book, you'll be considered an expert in your field, the media will be interested in you, and your customers and prospects have an opportunity to get to know your philosophy in a low risk fashion.

Your book can become a high class brochure for your business and a powerful way to establish your credibility in your marketplace.

However, before you pull out a notebook and start writing, let's spend a few moments on some of the barriers that may prevent you from getting your book out of your head and into the hands of your readers.

Section 1

Seven Strategy Barriers

What are Strategy Barriers?

◇◇

These barriers revolve around the 'how' of writing a book. Once you understand the strategies that successful authors employ, these barriers evaporate.

Barrier 1: I can't write well enough to be an author.

Do you have a Mrs. Farmer in your head?

Mrs. Farmer was my 4th grade teacher. She was very intelligent, quick, and easily frustrated. Her blue eyes would turn icy whenever a student was lazy or careless. Nobody wanted to get onto her bad side.

I can still hear her telling me that I had sloppy handwriting, terrible spelling, and poor grammar. In all fairness, Mrs. Farmer was a good teacher but her criticism stayed in my mind much longer than her praise.

You undoubtedly have memories of stinging criticism from a parent or teacher lurking in your memory bank as well. Those memories materialize whenever you think about writing your book.

Other old memories from school days also chime in, reminding you that

- You can't spell

- Diagramming sentences makes you want to pull out your fingernails
- You never really can remember all those rules about when to use commas
- You can't image your way out of a cardboard box, let alone have enough creativity to figure out what goes into a two hundred page book

Who do you hear in your mind telling you that you can't write?

Describe who that person was in your life, what age you were when you knew that person, and list the words of criticism that stung.

Remember that you're grown now. Resolve to show that old so-and-so and write a great book, just to prove that you can!

Barrier 2: It will take me too long and cost too much money to write my book

While the first barrier concerned your past, this one projects you into a scary future. It paints a picture of years of lonely toil, struggling over each word.

Like the character Jack in The Shining, we imagine ourselves slowing losing our grip on reality and typing the same word over and over as our family life falls apart.

We are so good at scaring ourselves!

We think that writing a book will mean that we have to quit our jobs, close our businesses, and become hermits.

Then, we scare ourselves further by deciding that our book will cost tens of thousands of dollars to publish and sell. We predict a confusing process of seeking a publisher or struggling through the steps of self publishing. We fear sinking our meager savings into a book, leaving us old and penniless.

What if we used that same level of creativity to create a vision of book success instead of terrifying nightmare?

Go ahead; write your most frightening book horror story here. Get it all out your system in gory detail.

My book nightmare..........

Now, read your writing. Notice that none of your story is based in fact.

Since you are just making up a story, write a triumphant story instead.

Paint a glorious picture of literary success, words flowing effortlessly from your fingers, and international acclaim.

My book success story....

Andrea Lee, is a busy entrepreneur with several businesses and more websites than I can count. She wrote her last book, <u>Money, Meaning and Beyond</u>, with her co-author Tina Forsyth in forty-five days. Tina had just given birth to her first child and Andrea continued to run her multiple businesses. If these busy women can write a book that quickly, what can you do?

Many authors routinely write books in ninety days.

You can select a time line for your book that makes sense for your busy life. It is possible to be a part- time writer and create excellent books, especially when you are writing non-fiction business building books.

Barrier 3: The Mechanics of Writing Are Beyond Me

This barrier reminds you that you don't have a degree in journalism or creative writing, that you never know when to use a semi colon, and that you've never read the Chicago Manual of Style.

Guess what?

Every author has an editor. It's the editor's job to take your writing and polish it up. Dan Brown, Stephen Covey, Nora Roberts, Harvey McKay, and all your favorite authors rely on editors.

Think about bestselling books by Bill Clinton, Rudy Giuliani, and Paris Hilton. Do you really think they wrote their books without an editor's assistance?

An author communicates ideas.

You have lots of ideas.

Work from your strengths. If you don't enjoy putting words on paper, hire someone to interview you or use voice recognition software.

The most successful non-fiction books are written in a conversational tone, not high brow academic language. In fact, writers like Malcolm Gladwell, author of <u>Blink</u> and <u>The Tipping Point</u>, are celebrated because they can take complex data and express it in a simple, understandable fashion.

You can do that too!

What do you write today?

Can you save great emails, recycle articles, or use information from a presentation you've created?

Barrier 4: My book has to be perfect or it is a failure

When you write your book, your inner perfectionist may freak out. I worked with an author who struggled for seven years to write her book because she was determined that every word would be perfect.

No book is totally flawless. Books published by the most respected publishing houses in New York still have a typographical error or two. I read a book a couple of years ago by one of the best selling authors in the world and found that the heroine's name was switched to Angela in one paragraph. Another author was mortified when the word public was misprinted as pubic in his footnotes.

Certainly it is important that you write a book that represents you professionally in the marketplace. However, no matter how hard you try and how often your book is edited, there may still be an error or two.

When you spot those errors, you can easily correct them in the next printing.

If you concentrate on communicating your message in a perfectly clear fashion, your book will serve your readers well and help you grow your business.

That's the type of perfectionism to strive for in your book!

****

NOTE: Grammatical purists would rephrase that sentence to read-

That is the type of perfectionism for which you should strive in your book.

Few people speak so formally. Which sentence sounds more friendly and conversational to you?

Barrier 5: There are too many books about my topic on the market already

This barrier makes you think that your knowledge isn't worthy or as important as someone else's ideas. Don't listen when it whispers things like

- Other people have written books about this topic
- I don't know anything new or revolutionary
- People don't read books any more
- My ideas aren't worthy

Coach Flo Schell wanted to write a book on selling. If she let this barrier stop her, she would have told herself that there were already hundreds of books on selling so her book wasn't needed.

However, Flo's book, <u>Stop Selling...Start Clicking</u>, presents the art of selling in a heart centered way, based on her many years of experience in selling educational services and franchises. During the course of her career, Flo was able to observe numerous selling successes and failures. She developed a process based on those observations. No one else but Flo could have written that book. Her experiences were her best teachers.

The next time you are at the mall, go into a bookstore. Stroll the aisles and notice how many books are written on cooking, parenting, accounting, auto repair, marketing, or home decorating. Each book presents information in a slightly different way, from a slightly different perspective.

Your book will present information that you've learned and experienced. No one else has lived your life. Therefore, no one else can write the same book that you can write.

Grab your pen and answer these questions:

What questions do my friends, clients, customers, or family members routinely ask me?

What problems have I overcome?

What experiences were my greatest learning opportunities?

Answering these questions will help you get in touch with the one-of-a-kind flavor that you can bring to your book.

The most successful books include stories. Adults like to be entertained while they learn.

Only you can tell the story of the time you blew up your computer, the day you ran your car into a tree, or what you learned about business from your grandfather.

While you write your book, pepper it with a few stories to illustrate your point.

Then, you'll have a book that stands out in the marketplace because it contains a spark of you.

There's one other important point to consider here. This barrier will entice you to forget that people are hungry for information. Small business owners read scores of books on business success. People who enjoy self-help books read many of them. My husband has a whole library of home repair books. I hate to admit that I have more cookbooks than I can fit into one book case.

When people are passionate about a topic, they consume many books in that area. To an avid business person, self development fan, devoted parent, or cooking enthusiast, if each book presents just one fresh idea, it is a success.

The same theory will apply to your book.

Barrier 6: To write a book, I have to know what I stand for and I'm not sure I really know what I stand for.

This one is hogwash.

If you are anything like me, you have plenty of opinions. Just ask your spouse or your kids.

Passion sells. So does controversy.

Dan Brown's book, <u>The Da Vinci Code</u>, sold millions of copies based on a controversial approach to a generally accepted belief.

I'm not suggesting that you create a controversy just to stir up trouble. However, if you select a topic that you are interested in, the process of putting your book together will naturally result in clarifying your opinion of that topic.

When you select your book topic, choose to write about something that you believe in, something you know that will help others, or something that will help your business stand out in the marketplace.

Don't pick a topic that bores you.

By the time you finish your book, you will have spent hours thinking even more deeply about your topic. Your ideas will be reinforced and clarified. You'll find yourself speaking easily and eloquently about your topic.

That's one of the unexpected benefits of writing your book.

Enjoy!

Barrier 7: I don't know where to start

This statement may feel like the truth for now.

Writing a book is a large project. It is easy to feel overwhelmed and quit before you really get a good start.

It may seem difficult to envision your finished book or the steps you need to complete it.

However……

Can you put words on paper?

Can you write emails?

Can you remember how to create a simple outline?

Can you follow a recipe or use a roadmap?

Writing a non-fiction book is a project. There is a system to completing it easily and rapidly. The process of writing a book has a beginning, middle, and an end, just like every other project you've ever completed.

The first time you tried to parallel park your car, you needed a little guidance. The first time you tried to use a new DVD player, plant a garden, or use a Stairmaster at the gym, you needed a little guidance. Things are only hard until you do them. Then, they seem easy.

Writing your first book will be a bit of a challenge because you've not done it before. However, there is a wealth of resources for aspiring authors. You can read books, take classes, join writers' groups, or attend writing conferences. You can hire a writing coach or book shepherd. You can even work with a ghost writer or co-writer.

Once you allow yourself to be a beginner and search out the information you need to begin, you will see that this barrier is an invitation to learn a new skill.

Section 2

Beliefs

What Are My Belief Barriers?

The barriers in this section are more subtle than the barriers relating to strategies. These barriers deal with your internal mindset and beliefs.

Your mind thinks up to 50,000 thoughts each day. Many of these thoughts rest just under the surface of your conscious awareness. Yet, their impact is felt in every choice that you make.

Beliefs about writing a book are slippery. Some may seem very recognizable to you. Others will seem untrue.

My experience is that all writers encounter all these common beliefs about writing. These barriers lead to procrastination, confusion about what topic to pursue and feelings of being overwhelmed.

When you examine these beliefs closely, you'll notice they all center on lack and fear.

Once you recognize that you are being controlled by lack and fear, you can decide to shift your thinking.

When you start believing all the reasons why you CAN write your book, all these beliefs regarding why you can't write will evaporate.

Barrier 8: I'm not smart or degreed enough

This barrier doesn't whisper. It shouts.

You may hear a litany of doubts about your suitability to write your book.

They may sound like:

- I don't know enough about this subject
- People won't take me seriously if I don't have a PhD
- Everyone knows this information already
- My business is too new for me to write a book
- I'm too young or too old
- No one has given me permission to become an expert on this topic
- I got poor grades in school, especially in English

Who am I to Write a Book

All these beliefs can be summarized in one phrase, "Who am I to write a book?"

This is the key belief that prevents you from writing a book. When you can conquer this belief, you can overcome all the other barriers with ease.

It may help to know that all writers hear these internal doubts. In fact, all of us have similar doubts whenever we try something new or create a goal that stretches us.

The best way to master this self-doubt is to stop thinking about you. Instead, focus on how the information in your book will help the people who read it.

There is an exercise that I teach all of my writing students and book coaching clients. Completing it will help you shift your thinking away from your feelings of lack and point them towards your desire to help others.

Try this exercise and repeat it whenever you feel that you are not worthy of writing a book.

Think of a time when you read a book that changed your life in some way.

What book was it?

How did reading that book influence you?

Did that book give you comfort, inspiration, information, or a smile?

Can you recall your feelings of anticipation before you read that book? Were you thinking, "This is the answer I've been looking for"? Or, were you surprised that the book left such a lasting impression on you?

Now, think about the book that you want to write. What problem will it solve for your reader?

How will the information in your book help your readers?

What action do you want your readers to take after they complete your book?

How will taking that action make a difference in the life of your reader?

Imagine your future reader closing your book and saying, "Now I know exactly what to do to help me with_____."

Whenever you feel doubts about your authority, worthiness, or talent, shift your thinking to all the ways that the information in your book will help your reader. Return to that scene that you just visualized and drink in the gratitude your reader will have for your book and for you.

Then, get busy and start writing!

Barrier 9

Who am I to tell other people what to do?

The belief barrier waves all your shortcomings in your face.

It reminds you that your life/business/health/whatever is not perfect. It falsely tells you that if people knew what you were *really* like they would call you a fraud. According to this barrier, you are a long way from being a guru.

When you experience these kinds of thoughts, examine them by answering these questions:

Who is my favorite author?

Do I think he is perfect?

Do I care about the condition of her bank account, basement, thighs, or parenting style OR do I care about the information I get from her books?

People read books for information and inspiration.

When your write a Business Building Book sharing your knowledge and experiences, you are not claiming perfection. You are simply sharing information.

Consider yourself a reporter, researcher, or guide who is helping someone avoid painful mistakes or reach a goal faster. Actually, most of us prefer to learn from real people who have struggled with some of the same problems we face every day.

Oprah Winfrey, Abraham Lincoln, and Nelson Mandela are admired because they lived an imperfect life and triumphed.

We believe that Bill Gates is shy and geeky. Sharing that human side makes his success more inspiring. We know he did not become a success based on his good looks or suave style. Oprah is admired because she doesn't try to cover up her humble origins or weight issues.

The most powerful business books share the story of your journey, including your mistakes, blunders, and on-going challenges. Overcoming obstacles makes you human and admirable.

Instead of fearing your shortcomings, embrace them, and where appropriate, include them in your book. Doing so will help your readers believe your information and trust that you've walked the same path that they are walking today.

Barrier 10
Writing is hard and lonely

Do you imagine yourself locked away in a seedy hotel room or a remote cabin, feverishly writing your book?

It is easy to believe the story that writing a book requires suffering, pain, and isolation. In fact, you may believe that the harder you struggle to write your book, the better it will be.

Nonsense.

While you will require periods of peace and quiet to write your book, there is no law that says you have to live in a lonely garret and waste away while you are writing it.

In fact, when you are writing a business building book, you will want to spend plenty of time with other people. Market research can be fun and very interactive.

Let's say that you are a parenting coach who is writing a book on parenting techniques for mothers of elementary school students. If you want to write an outstanding parenting book, it would only make sense to get to know some mothers at the PTA, playground, or soccer practice to learn about the challenges mothers face.

If you are writing a book for small business owners to grow your marketing business, participating in networking groups, business forums, and conferences will give you a keen insight into the needs of your readers.

When you select the group for whom you will write your book, spend time with them. Ask them questions, get feedback on ideas, and inquire if they would like to be formally interviewed for your book.

This strategy gives you multiple benefits. First, it will erase your belief that you must write your book in lonely isolation, making the process much more enjoyable.

Secondly, you will gain valuable insight into the content of your book.

Lastly, you will be amazed at the warm reception you receive.

People admire authors. Most will be curious about what you are writing and be delighted to share their ideas with you. It is flattering to be interviewed for a book or to give feedback on a concept.

The positive feedback you get from others will encourage you to continue with your book project.

The more you talk about your book with potential readers, the more accurate your book will be, the more you will enjoy the process of writing it, and the more eager buyers you will have when the book is published.

Who are your target readers?

Who do you currently know that fits the profile of your intended reader?

Where can you easily network with other future readers? (Consider online networking as well as face to face networking)

Could you conduct a survey, take an informal poll or find ways to better understand the needs of your future readers?

Barrier 11: No one but my mother will read my book

People today are hungry for information, especially information that is quickly accessible and useful.

The internet taught our generation that you can find answers to your challenges in written form. As a society, we believe that answers can be found in a book or a website. We are no longer content to accept our fate; we want to make our lives better.

According to the Association of American Publishers, book sales increased by 9.9 percent from 2004-2005. People in the United States bought 25.1 billion dollars worth of books in 2005.

These facts dispel the myth that people don't read books any more. Check out the full report of the sales data at http://www.publishers.org/industry/index.cfm

Do you read books?

If so, you are accustomed to seeking solutions and information via the printed word. Many people in our society are visual learners who retain written information well.

You are not writing your book for everyone in the world. You are writing your book to help a distinct group of people solve a problem. Why wouldn't they want to find the solution to that problem in your book?

Additionally, once you write your book, you can create CDs, teleclasses, or workshops with the same material. In that way, you will be able to present your information in a way that all learners, visual, auditory, and kinesthetic, will be able to enjoy.

When you create a well written book and a savvy marketing plan, you will be delighted by all the people who want to read your book.

P.S. Moms can be great proof readers... mine is!

Barrier 12: I'll be ridiculed and humiliated if I write this book.

This belief barrier sounds amusing when you read it. However, for some people, it feels very real.

If your book will create controversy or topple a widely accepted belief, it may ruffle a few feathers. However, since the aim of your book is to build your business, you can create a book that appeals to your current customers.

If you have clients or customers who benefit from your work today, it is only logical that you will be able to create a book that will benefit others.

People are no longer burned at the stake for proposing new ideas.

Conducting your market research will help you write a desirable book.

Any fears about your writing style can be allayed with the help of a good editor.

There is nothing to fear- your book will help your career, not hurt it, especially if you learn how to create it strategically.

Barrier 13

I'll become famous and be overwhelmed by reporters and paparazzi who will stalk my every move for the morning papers.

Most of us struggle with a fear of success just as much as a fear of failure. When this belief barrier activates in your mind, you can quickly create an overwhelming fantasy. It's a good fantasy but it is a bit frightening as well.

Your mind paints a picture of rapid success, news trucks in your front yard, and grueling multi-city book tours that take you away from your family for months on end.

What would you say to your client or your friend if he were talking this way?

If your book becomes an instant success- great! You can handle it.

More likely, your book will become a gradual success over time.

The remedy to this belief barrier is to set clear goals for your book.

Ask yourself:

What outcome do I want for this book?

How will it contribute to my business?

Will it be a method of lead generation, a way to extend the number of people I can help, or a product that will generate passive revenue or customer loyalty?

How does this book align with my company goals?

When you create a clear-cut strategy for your business building book, your fear will evaporate. With a firm plan and destination in mind, you can write your book and manage its growth.

However, if Oprah calls, go, even if you have to cancel a few meetings!

Solutions and Strategies

Strategies You Can Use

Now that you've examined all the barriers that could stop you from writing your book, let's review some strategies you can use to make the process of creating your book easier.

Strategy 1

Get support

Writing a book is a big project. Any time that you begin something new and challenging, you benefit from support.

During the writing process, you will need several types of support.

First, you need someone who can help you with the mechanics of writing your book logically and clearly. You can take a writing class, participate in a writers' circle, or talk about your book with a friend who has writing skills. When you have someone who can show you the ropes, writing is not so difficult.

Next, you need gentle nagging. Ask someone you trust to help you stay on task and encourage you not to quit. Enlist a writing coach, trusted friend, spouse, or family member.

Be sure to ask for their support at the beginning of your book project. Then, when you are frustrated and feeling like shelving the project, call that person and ask for some encouragement.

Finally, get some support in your professional circles. Talk with your clients, customers, and members of your network about your book project. The more people that you tell about your book, the more excitement you will enjoy. When someone asks you how your book is progressing, you'll be even more motivated to complete it.

Think about the people that you know.

Who can provide you with support on the mechanics of writing?

Which close friends or relatives will be happy to provide you with gentle nagging and enthusiastic support?

Which close friends or relatives will laugh at your idea?

Note: Do not mention your book to this group until it is finished!

Which of your customers or professional contacts would like to hear about your book and be interested in its progress?

Strategy 2
Set a date publicly. Be bold.

Set a date when you hope to have your book completed and share it with others.

Announce, "I'm writing a book and plan to have it completed within the next ____ months."

Making a public commitment takes courage. However, it also cements the goal in your mind and gives you a clear time frame for completion.

Certainly, you want to set a realistic date. Give yourself enough time to write the book while you live the rest of your life. Get out your calendar and record that date.

Then, schedule time each week to work on your book. Schedule the time all the way to your completion date.

When you will commit time in your calendar for your book at the beginning of the writing process, you will be much more likely to complete your project.

Public commitments and private time management skills are two vital ways to provide the structure you need to complete your book.

Strategy 3: Write daily

Begin to write for enjoyment today.

Create a blog, start a journal, write short articles or tips lists.

Writing well is a skill that can be learned and developed. The more frequently you write, the more natural and easy it will become for you.

For an excellent discussion on developing your writing muscles, read <u>The Artist's Way</u> by Julia Cameron. This wonderful book will inspire you to write daily and provide many exercises to use to develop your skill.

Strategy 4: Read great books

Good writers are readers. The more you read, the easier it will be for you to write well.

Go to your local library and find the writing section. There will be a wealth of books sharing writing tips.

Next, go to the business section. Read some best selling business books. When you read them, notice the tone of the writing.

In the most popular non-fiction books, the tone is friendly and conversational, without complicated sentences and difficult vocabulary.

In fact, the most successful business books make complex information easy to understand. <u>Good to Great</u> by Jim Collins, <u>Blink</u> by Malcolm Gladwell and <u>A Whole New Mind</u> by Daniel Pink are examples of bestselling books written in a conversational tone.

Finally, go to the section of the library where your target readers find books. Look at some of the other books on your subject. Notice which books look worn. These are the most frequently read books.

Examine these popular books. Notice the cover, the table of contents, and the copy on the back cover.

These well worn and best loved books reveal what your readers want. Decide which of those elements you want to use in your book.

Do the same research on Amazon. Check out the best selling books in your topic area. Notice the pricing, read the publisher's information and the reviews. Learn all you can about what your ideal readers are buying and reading.

This market research will help you write an appealing book.

Strategy 5: Understand the publishing process

While you are writing your book, it will help to know what happens to your manuscript after you have it completed.

The publishing process can seem confusing and complicated. Let me give you a high level overview of how books are transformed from rough drafts into finished form.

First, your rough draft will be edited for clarity of content and grammatical style.

The publisher will assign an ISBN number, which is similar to a Social Security Number for books. The publisher also sets the retail and wholesale price of your book.

Next, it will be typeset or arranged on the page in a stylized book format, using certain fonts, headers and footers, and other graphic design elements so it will be easy and enjoyable to read.

Then, a cover designer will create a compelling cover, using your ideas and the sales copy you create for your back cover. The cover designer will also create a bar code and insert it into the back cover.

After a final proof read, the cover and typeset book will be sent to a printer who produces a hard or soft cover version of your book.

Then, your book is ready to be launched into the hands of your eager readers.

While this process may sound difficult, it is not.

You can choose to self-publish your book, use a small publishing house, or get an agent and seek publication by one of the major industry publishers.

At this point, all you need is the basic understanding of the publishing process. Once your book is written, you can explore the many options for transforming it into a physical book.

Strategy 6
Select your topic wisely

One of the most common questions I answer in emails and in my writing classes sounds like this, "I have so many ideas – how can I pick one that will become a successful book?"

Choosing a topic for your first book can seem like part market research, part divination, and part pure dumb luck. Some people get so bogged down when trying to pick a topic that they never get around to actually writing the book.

In the publishing world, the term *platform* identifies the reasons why an author is able to write credibly on a topic.

For example, a physician would have a strong platform to write a book on a health related topic but not on architecture. A professional speaker could have a strong platform for a book on effective communication, public speaking, overcoming fear, networking, as well as the topic of his or her presentations. A professional realtor could write a believable book on tips for first time home buyers. That same book, written by a car salesman, would not seem as credible.

What's your platform?

Many people who want to write a non-fiction book have already written other materials. To streamline the process of writing your book, take an inventory of things you've already created. You may find bits and pieces that you can weave into your book.

Next, create a profile of a perfect reader for your book. A perfect reader fits the description of your target market or ideal customer. Remember, the purpose of your book is to build your business, so write a book that will appeal to your favorite customers.

Review these fictional profiles to spark your thinking:

For a book written by a personal trainer:

Sue is a thirty-five-old married woman who lives in an upscale suburb. She is the proud parent of Keith, aged 11, who excels at basketball. Sue and her husband Ted hope that Keith will continue with basketball and earn a college scholarship. Sue and her husband both earn a good living and are committed to physical health. Active parents, they find time to attend all Keith's games and are willing to do what they can to support him in becoming the best he can be.

Book Topic- Nurturing your budding athlete

Business purpose- Enroll young teens in a speed and strength conditioning program

For a book written by a realtor:

Joanne is a fifty-four year old woman who recently divorced. She works as a nurse administrator at a local children's hospital. Her job is very stressful with unpredictable hours. Joanne has three adult children. She's spent the last fifteen years living in a four bedroom home in a prosperous area. She dislikes coming home to an empty house full of old memories.

Book topic- Selling your home without stress

Business purpose- List Joanne's current home and help her find a new residence more suited to her busy lifestyle.

For a book written by a marketing consultant:

Andrew is a forty-nine year old owner of an Italian restaurant. Andrew inherited this restaurant and his love of cooking from his immigrant parents and grew up in the business. He has a group of loyal customers who have been eating at his restaurant for many years. Several new office buildings have just been erected near his restaurant. Andrew is considering adding catering services but feels concerned about depleting his staff and financial resources.

Book topic- Decision making tips for small business owners

Business purpose- A consulting contract to conduct a feasibility study and possible marketing plan

When you have a similar profile of your perfect reader, it will be easy for you to choose a perfect book topic that will serve him or her.

Create a profile of your perfect reader, complete with name, family situation, occupation, age, and as many details as you can. Have fun with this! It's just like creating an imaginary friend. There are no wrong answers.

If you are unable to create a perfect reader for your book, use yourself.

If you are a fifty- year old white male, mid-level manager, married with three teens and a huge mortgage, who is a deacon in his church, and has a passion for bass fishing, you could write a great book on spirituality in corporate life, tips for new managers, stress management tips learned while fishing, talking to your teen, leadership, life balance, time management, or personal development for men.

However, be certain to select a book topic that can fit into your future business goals. You will be speaking, writing, and discussing the topic of your book for many years to come.

If you are a consultant who is feeling a bit bored with writing business plans and you write a book on business planning, you will be stuck with that topic for a long time.

Additionally, consider the longevity of your potential topic. In the writing world, this step is called choosing an 'evergreen' or 'hot' topic.

Some books are designed to have a short but important life span. These 'hot' books are written in response to current events.

For example, after the tragedy on September 11, 2001, many books were written on disaster preparedness. In ten years, that topic may not be popular, but those books were brisk sellers then.

'Evergreen' topics are universal issues that people face as part of the human or business experience, like topics on health, aging, relationships, business growth, career transition, leadership skills, time management, or parenting.

You can choose a topic that is based on a current need or an evergreen topic. Both options are worthy. The only difference is in the marketing approach you will take.

Finally, since this is your first book, stack the deck in your favor by choosing a topic that you enjoy and can easily complete. If you select a topic that feels difficult to write, and that requires many hours of research, it will take you far too long to complete it. Chances are, you will quit somewhere in the middle of the project.

Remember the ultimate goal for your book is building your business. By choosing a topic that you like and find easy, you are working from your natural strengths – always your most powerful position.

The Next Steps

So, are you convinced?

Do you feel confident that you can write a book and build your business?

I hope so!

Writing a book is a thrilling experience. Sure, it takes some hard work, but the joy you will feel when you hold your finished book in your hands makes it well worth the effort.

You CAN write a book that builds your business, garners media attention, shares your knowledge, and makes you an expert in your field.

The book you are holding in your hands is an example of a Business Building Book. I give this book away freely each time I do a presentation or meet someone who says he wants to write a book.

The purpose of this book is to inspire you to write a book and give you some information to help you understand the process.

At the same time, it builds a relationship with interested readers and demonstrates that I have useful knowledge and expertise.

Because it is a short book, it is easy to read and inexpensive to produce. In fact, each copy costs less than three dollars to print.

I share this information with you to demonstrate that writing a book is a smart business decision.

When you are ready to write your book, check the resources section for a variety of offerings that can help you.

Thank you for the time you spent reading this book. I hope it has been inspirational, informative, and empowering!

To your writing and business success,

Lynne Klippel
2007

Bibliography

Boress, Allan. *The I Hate Selling Book.* Kearney, NE: Morris Publishing, 1995.

Brown, Dan. *The DaVinci Code.* New York: Doubleday, 2003.

Cameron, Julia. *The Artist's Way.* New York: Tarcher, 1992.

Chicago Editorial Staff. *Chicago Manual of Style.* Chicago: University of Chicago Press, 2003 edition.

Collins, Jim. *Good to Great.* New York: HarperCollins, 2001.

Gladwell, Malcolm. *Blink.* New York: Little Brown, 2005.

_____. *The Tipping Point.* New York: Little Brown, 2000.

Lee, Andrea J. *Money, Meaning, and Beyond.* St. Peters, MO: MP Press, 2006.

Pink, Daniel. *A Whole New Mind.* New York: Penguin, 2005.

Schell, Flo. *Stop Selling…Start Clicking.* St. Peters, MO: MP Press, 2006.

Resources

Lynne Klippel and her publishing partner, best selling author Christine Kloser, have a veriety of resources available to help you write your Business Building Book, including a full service publishing company, coaching programs, educational materials, editing, cover design, and the award winning **Get Your Book Done®** program, the most comprehensive and successful writing program for Entraprenuial Authors available.

For a free audio with Lynne and Christine entitled, **How to Get Your Book Done Right**, visit LoveYourLifePublishing.com.

About the Author

Lynne Klippel got into heaps of trouble as a child for reading books when she was supposed to be doing chores.

Since then, she's worked as a teacher, librarian, researcher, coach, and health care professional. She holds a BS in Education and a MOT in Occupational Therapy.

Lynne wrote her first book in 2003 to build her coaching business. Since that time, she keeps busy with writing, teaching, publishing, consultation, and hosting an internet radio show, <u>Web Sorority Talk Radio</u>.

Lynne is a frequent presenter on the topic of writing and provides individual coaching and consulting on writing and publishing for small business owners.

Lynne lives in Missouri with her husband and business partner, Larry, three sons, a shaggy dog, an independent cat, and a very quiet lizard - whom she ignores.

www.ingramcontent.com/pod-product-compliance
Ingram Content Group UK Ltd.
Pitfield, Milton Keynes, MK11 3LW, UK
UKHW041412180426
11947UKWH00007B/91